METAVERSE

THE COMPLETE GUIDE TO INVESTING IN THE METAVERSE

Terence A. Cano

Contents

Chapter One

INTRODUCTION

It's the next huge technological breakthrough. It's all a joke. It's a marketing tactic. It's a dismal techno-dystopian nightmare. These are the thoughts of many people right now towards the metaverse. The metaverse can be defined as a virtual environment where people can connect, work, and play.

There are the obvious skippable ideas, the ones you eventually accept it's time to pay attention to, and the small basket of once-in-a-generation innovations that are so strong that they begin to exert gravitational pull-on numerous facets of our existence.

The metaverse has officially changed the game. Though still in its infancy, it's evident that the metaverse will drastically alter how we interact online, how companies advertise, how quickly crypto is accepted, and a variety of other aspects of life. Here's an explainer to help you grasp what's going on—and what's to come.

Although the term 'metaverse' became popular after Facebook, the well-known social platform changed its name to Meta last month, and many people are still unsure what it is and whether the futuristic, technical notion is something they should take seriously.

Some critics argue that by focusing on the metaverse and renaming itself while the company is dealing with a PR crisis, Facebook is diverting attention away from the real-world problems it causes or contributes to, such as harming teens' mental health, facilitating the spread of disinformation, and fueling political polarization.

According to internal business correspondence obtained by Recode, some Facebook employees are concerned about the metaverse, as seen by queries numerous employees posed ahead of a weekly staff Q&A on Facebook's internal messaging network, Workplace. One topic that received a lot of votes from employees was, how might we avoid a dystopian future in which the metaverse is utilized as 'opium for the masses?'

Another popular concern was how will we effectively prioritize safety, integrity, and accountability in the Metaverse? Today, we hardly have enough time to cover the actual world.

Other analysts have remarked that Facebook's metaverse concept isn't novel - several other businesses, including Roblox, Nvidia, and Microsoft, have been developing virtual worlds using virtual or augmented reality technology. Others point out how immature the technology is – in the version of the metaverse that Facebook has so far produced, the digital avatars it gives as stand-ins for our real bodies are cartoonish, clumsy, and frequently legless.

Even if these objections and issues are valid, Facebook's investment in the metaverse should be taken seriously. Mark Zuckerberg sees the metaverse as the successor to mobile internet, an innovation that altered all of our lives by allowing us to connect to the internet from any place and enabled Facebook's present business to exist. Suppose Zuckerberg's metaverse becomes what he wants it to be. In that case, it might similarly shake up the world, altering our existence from one based in our physical world to one in which our digital presence progressively complements our actual one.

In response to worries about the metaverse, Facebook, which just rebranded itself, Meta, cited a statement from a September post given by Facebook executives Andrew Bosworth and Nick Clegg, which stated, in part, Meta is not planning to construct, control, or govern the metaverse on its own. We're having early dialogues about our vision for the metaverse, even before some of the technologies are available. We're talking about it right now to make sure that any terms of service, privacy restrictions, or safety measures are appropriate for new technology and successful in keeping people safe.

Facebook has also stated that it does not intend to be the sole developer of the metaverse. This will not be the sole responsibility of any single corporation. To do it right, it will take collaboration across industries as well as with experts, governments, and regulators, says another passage from the blog post.

The corporation is placing a large stake in the success of this initiative. It is putting some of the world's greatest engineering minds to work on this project, purchasing virtual reality and augmented reality firms, recruiting over 10,000 people to work on it, and investing tens of billions of dollars in it. And Zuckerberg, who has ultimate authority over his firm, appears to be really pleased about it.

While the timetable is still unknown, it's probable that we'll all be utilizing some yet-to-be- determined form of the metaverse to connect to the internet in the future. And Facebook is keen to play a big part in creating and molding this new environment, which means that even if Facebook does not solely own the metaverse (as it has stated), it is nonetheless attempting to exert influence over it. As a result, Facebook may one day have even greater power over our everyday lives.

Today, Facebook must still operate under the constraints imposed by Apple and Google, which create and run the world's major smartphone operating systems. However, in this new world, which will most likely rely on VR/AR headsets and digital sensors, Facebook is attempting to develop its own set of rules and operating platform.

Even if you have no plans to enter the metaverse anytime soon, you should keep an eye on it and how Facebook is investing in it.

ORIGIN AND DEFINITION OF METAVERSE

Chapter Two

ROLE OF FACEBOOK IN METAVERSE

What Is the Origin of The Term Metaverse?

According to Fortune's Jonathan Vanian, the term metaverse was used by Neal Stephenson in his science-fiction novel Snow Crash to allude to a digital cosmos that may be explored through virtual reality. It's a common story device in many modern works of science fiction, including the Matrix films and the novel and film Ready Player One.

What Is Metaverse?

For decades, the incredible potential of virtual worlds was only imagined in science fiction novels. Today, the term metaverse is one of the most popular in the computer world, and it is being warmly adopted by software and game creators in a variety of industries, from crypto and gaming to social media. The metaverse has evolved into a very real phenomenon, with a slew of thriving platforms boasting ever-increasing crypto integrations.

8 METAVERSE

Everyone seems to be talking about the Metaverse as the next big thing that will change our online life these days. Everyone appears to have their own version of the Metaverse if they have one at all.

The word metaverse was used in Neal Stephenson's seminal cyberpunk novel Snow Crash, which was released in 1992. But what exactly is the Metaverse? The Metaverse (always capitalized in Stephenson's fiction) is portrayed as a shared imaginary realm that is made available to the public through the worldwide fiber-optics network and projected onto virtual reality goggles in the novel. As a result, the word can refer to digital environments that have been supplemented using virtual reality (VR) or augmented reality (AR).

The term meta means beyond, and the poem alludes to the universe. Furthermore, some individuals use the word metaverse to refer to virtual worlds in which players may walk around and interact with other players, such as a world in which developers can design buildings, parks, signs, and other things that do not exist in reality. It has massive floating overhead light shows as well as noteworthy communities (where the rules of three-dimensional spacetime are ignored, and free-combat zones where people can go hunting and kill each other).

The COVID-19 outbreak sparked curiosity in the metaverse. As more people work and go to school online, there is a greater need for methods to make online communication more lifelike.

Nick, the two largest metaverse platforms, the Sandbox and Decentraland, each has a finite number of plots of land, and both have said that they would never generate more.

Some significant adjustments support the debut of these new platforms.

According to The Information, we are reaching the conclusion of Web 2.0 and entering the dawn of Web 3.0, also known as the metaverse, after a 15-year run. Three major forces are pushing this: the emergence of cryptocurrency, the apparent imminence of the experiential web via augmented and virtual reality, and a cultural shift hastened by COVID, which has encouraged individuals to connect and communicate in virtual environments.

In July 2021, Mark Zuckerberg said that the firm plans to build a more maximalist version of Facebook that encompasses social presence, office work, and entertainment. On October 28, 2021, Facebook changed its name to Meta, indicating its more serious commitment to developing a virtual world known as a metaverse.

Is The Metaverse Only a Facebook Project?

No, the Metaverse isn't merely a Facebook project. Microsoft and Nvidia, a chipmaker, are two more companies that are supporting the metaverse. Video gaming companies are also taking the lead. Epic Games, the creator of the popular video game Fortnite, has raised $1 billion in funding from investors to support its long-term metaverse ambitions.

Another major gaming platform participant, Roblox, characterizes the metaverse as a place where people may join together within millions of 3D experiences to learn, work, play, create, and interact.

Consumer companies are seeking to cash in on the trend as well. Gucci, an Italian fashion house, collaborated with Roblox in June to launch a range of digital-only accessories. Coca-Cola and Clinique both offered digital tokens touted as a means of entering the metaverse.

What Role Does Facebook Play in The Metaverse?

The firm is simply one of many players vying to conquer the metaverse, but it has lofty goals. And, early this year, it doubled down on its investments by legally changing its name to Meta. As Fortune put it: According to Zuckerberg, the metaverse is the next step in social networking, moving beyond static user profiles that allow individuals to just submit comments and photographs. People would need to wear VR headsets or augmented reality glasses to get there, which would superimpose the digital environment over the actual world. Lifelike holograms might likewise be projected into the actual world by cutting-edge projection devices.

On a conceptual level, as articulated by Zuckerberg and others, the metaverse is a method for us to combine our virtual and real lives more fluidly. It would seem like we're right there with people no matter how far off we actually are, and we'll be able to express ourselves in new delightful, truly immersive ways, Zuckerberg stated in an October lecture in which he demonstrated his metaverse vision.

The goal is to build a more immersive internet, in which we will spend more time interacting in virtual environments and experiences rather than the actual world, using technology such as AR and VR.

Right now, the internet is essentially something that is 'push,' stated Matthew Ball, a technology investor who produced a classic series of articles about the metaverse, to me. You have material pushed to you, you get an email, you get a notice, and you pull out your smartphone to retrieve it. The metaverse differs in that it is an embodied engine that you are already within, rather than seeking out, according to Ball.

In practice, this implies that we will be disconnected from our physical realities: the office, the living room, and the outdoors. Instead, we'll put on our headphones or otherwise immerse ourselves in another environment.

Depending on how you look at it, that may be an enhancement in your life; your surroundings or physical appearance can be virtually updated. It may also be viewed as a dystopian idea, as

though the metaverse is for individuals who want to escape the harsh realities of the actual world, which is how it was envisioned in the novel Snow Crash.

For the time being, however, any discussion of the metaverse is entirely speculative. Facebook will be the first to admit that it is still in its early stages. Zuckerberg has stated that it doesn't really exist yet and that we just have building blocks such as Facebook's Oculus Quest 2 headgear, which costs $299 and drastically lowers the entry price point for VR devices. In comparison, an HP Reverb G2 Virtual Reality Headset costs $450, while the HTC Vive Cosmos costs around $600.

PRIMARY CHARACTERISTICS OF A METAVERSE

What Are the Primary Characteristics of a Metaverse?

Science fiction has given rise to the most common concepts concerning the Metaverse. In this perspective, the Metaverse is commonly portrayed as a form of digital hacked-in internet — a depiction of true reality but anchored in a virtual (often theme park-like) universe. As a result, the Metaverse's basic characteristics are as follows:

Chapter Three

WHAT METAVERSE IS NOT

Synchronous and live: While pre-planned and self-contained events will take place, the Metaverse will be a living experience that occurs continually for everyone and in real-time, exactly like real life.

Persistent: It never resets, pauses, or ends but just continues indefinitely.

Individually and concurrently available: Everyone may be a member of the Metaverse and participate in a certain event/place/activity at the same time and with their agency in the Metaverse.

A fully functional economy: People and businesses should be able to create, own, invest

in, sell, and be reimbursed for a wide range of actions that provide value that others recognize.

A diverse set of contributors: It should be packed with material and experiences created and operated by a diverse set of contributors, some of whom are self-employed, while others run informally structured or commercially-oriented enterprises.

Provide unparalleled interoperability: It should provide exceptional data, digital items/assets, content, and other interoperability across each of the experiences—for example, a vehicle created for Rocket League (or even Porsche's website) may be transferred over to operate in Roblox. Today's digital world functions similarly to a shopping mall, with each store having its own money, unique ID cards, proprietary units of measurement for commodities such as shoes or calories, and distinct dress codes, among other things.

Is There Something Wrong with The Metaverse?

While not commonly acknowledged, a few more principles may be crucial to the Metaverse. One of these questions is whether users will have a unified digital identity (or avatar) that they would use in all of their interactions. This might be beneficial, but it's unlikely since each of the Metaverse age leaders will still want their identifying systems.

There are a few major account systems now, for example, but none spans the full web, and they usually stack atop one another with restricted data sharing/access. For example, if your iPhone is linked to an iOS account, you may check in to an app that is tied to your Gmail account using your Meta (formerly Facebook) ID.

There's also a dispute over how much interoperability is necessary for a metaverse to be the actual Metaverse rather than simply a development of the internet as we know it today. Many people also wonder if a true Metaverse can contain only one operator (as is the case in Ready Player One).

Some claim that the concept of a Metaverse requires a highly decentralized platform built mostly on community-driven standards and protocols (akin to the open web) and an open-source Metaverse OS or platform (though this does not rule out the presence of dominant closed platforms in the Metaverse).

What Is the Metaverse Not?

While the analogies above are most likely part of the Metaverse, they are not the Metaverse.

Virtual worlds and games featuring artificial intelligence (AI)-driven characters, as well as those inhabited in real-time with genuine humans, have existed for decades. As a result, a virtual world is not a meta-universe but rather a false and synthetic one developed for a specific purpose (a game).

Likewise, digital content experiences such as Second Life are sometimes referred to as proto- Metaverses.

However, some aspects of virtual worlds, such as the portrayal of humans by digital avatars, the lack of game-like goals or skill systems, and virtual hangouts endure, and although offering almost instantaneous new updates; they are insufficient for the Metaverse. As a result, virtual space is not a metaverse.

Virtual reality (VR) is a means of immersing oneself in a virtual world or environment. A sensation of presence in a digital environment is insufficient to define a metaverse. Furthermore, while a metaverse may have certain game-like goals, incorporate games, and employ gamification, it is not a game in and of itself, nor is it centered on specific goals. As a result, it's neither virtual reality nor a game.

A metaverse, unlike Disneyland, is not centrally planned; hence, it is not a virtual theme park. A metaverse, meanwhile, is not a new app store; rather, it is fundamentally distinct from current internet/mobile paradigms, design, and objectives.

HOW METAVERSE FUNCTION AND ITS OPTIONS

How Does the Metaverse Function?

In general, the metaverse may be classified into two types of platforms.

The first entails using nonfungible tokens (NFTs) and cryptocurrencies to launch blockchain- based metaverse enterprises. On the Decentral and The Sandbox platforms, users may purchase virtual land and design their own settings.

The second group uses the term metaverse to refer to virtual worlds in general, where individuals may interact for business or pleasure. Facebook Inc. announced the launch of a metaverse product team in July.

Despite the fact that many metaverse sites provide free accounts, anyone who buys or sells virtual goods on blockchain-based platforms must utilize cryptocurrency. Some blockchain- based platforms, like Decentral and's MANA and The Sandbox's SAND, require Ethereum- based crypto tokens to buy and sell virtual assets.

In Decentral and, users may exchange NFT artworks or charge for attendance at a virtual event or concert. They can also gain money by exchanging land, which has increased in value significantly in recent years. Users on Roblox may make money by charging other users for access to their games.

What Are Your Options in The Metaverse?

One may embark on a virtual trip, buy digital apparel, and attend a virtual performance in the crypto metaverse initiatives. In the midst of the COVID-19 epidemic, the Metaverse might be a game-changer for work-from-home shifts. Horizon Workrooms, a Facebook free open beta, is now available for download on Oculus Quest 2 in locations where Quest 2 is supported.

Workrooms are virtual meeting area that enables you and your colleagues to interact more efficiently from anywhere. You may attend a virtual conference as an avatar or make a video call

from your laptop or PC to the virtual room. You may use a large virtual whiteboard to work on ideas, bring your computer and keyboard into VR to interact with others, or conduct expressive talks that feel more like you're in person.

However, technology companies must still find out how to integrate their numerous online channels. To make it function, rival technical platforms must agree on a set of standards to prevent jumping between the Facebook metaverse, the Microsoft metaverse, and others.

Crypto Metaverse

A crypto metaverse is a virtual environment that uses blockchain technology and cryptocurrencies to provide an immersive experience. Crypto metaverses are virtual worlds that have enormous social and commercial possibilities.

Crypto metaverses can provide people with new opportunities to play, invest, collect, and communicate – as well as earn money from it all. Furthermore, although progress on the different unique metaverse platforms is notable, the numerous metaverse games can connect and interoperate with one another that has the potential to propel the nascent blockchain gaming ecosystem into a pillar of the global economy. Metaverse games are positioned to become a major part of the next phase of the internet by merging the immersive surroundings of VR, the addictive playability of video games, the interaction of social media, and the value propositions of cryptocurrency.

Features of Crypto Metaverse

Crypto metaverse creators have often endeavored to differentiate their worlds from previous generations of metaverses in three crucial ways:

Decentralization: Unlike early virtual worlds, which were owned and controlled by corporations, crypto metaverses are often decentralized, with some or all metaverse game components based on blockchain technology. As a result, blockchain metaverses tend to deviate

from today's game industry's mainstream corporate structures and value extraction strategies. The unique structure of blockchain games can provide participants with more equitable involvement options. It also implies that individuals in the metaverse share ownership of the metaverse. Even if the metaverse blockchain's original designers abandoned the project, the game might continue to exist indefinitely.

Provable provenance: Crypto tokens, such as non-fungible tokens, are used to represent in-world things in crypto metaverses (NFTs). Achievements and purchases in gaming environments can be quite valuable to players. NFTs modernize in-game item standards by providing much-needed openness and access to asset markets.

Real-world economic value: Because crypto metaverses employ cryptocurrency tokens and blockchain infrastructure, their economies are inextricably linked to the larger crypto economy.

Is Crypto the Metaverse's Key?

The purpose of the Metaverse is to give individuals an augmented reality experience that, in many respects, may outperform actual reality in terms of experiences and possibilities.

Let's look at why the metaverse needs encryption to work properly.

Blockchain's immutability is a crucial feature for any virtual reality platform to acquire widespread acceptance. Hacks and data breaches are routine, but if individuals are to function totally online and virtual, the fundamental platform on which they will operate must be safe.

Blockchain enables quick information confirmation and enables cryptographically safe and secured transactions.

Blockchain and crypto assets are critical components of how virtual reality will be deployed.

Continuing from the preceding point, the Metaverse will desire and require transactions to be completed on demand, which blockchain and crypto assets may assist in enabling. Transactions are required for a realistic virtual reality environment to function and execute as advertised.

These transfers must be safe and almost instantaneous. Individuals in this ecosystem will need to be able to:

transact and engage as easily as if they were in person,

and trust that these transactions will be completed.

Chapter Four

THE METAVERSE'S CRYPTO GUIDE

Crypto transactions, which are viable and established technologies, allow individuals and institutions to make transactions virtual, traceable, and real-time. However, even if blockchain and crypto-asset technologies are not used indefinitely, the trend toward virtual and online payments is expanding. Transacting and engaging in business online has become a mainstream progression, which has grown even more prevalent with the introduction of cryptocurrency payments by Visa, Mastercard, and PayPal.

Crypto-enabled payments become even more common in a virtual environment, such as the metaverse, and it stands to reason that such payments will continue to rise to prominence in the future.

The Metaverse is still a new and quickly growing field. To enable and realize a fully working metaverse, blockchain and crypto assets will need to play a substantial role in its future implementation.

CHAPTER ONE

Investing in metaverse

We will talk about metaverse currencies, tokens, wallets, blockchain metaverse businesses, crypto metaverse initiatives, and how the metaverse works in this book.

A metaverse is a shared, immersive virtual world where participants, usually represented by avatars, can interact with one another, create in-world objects and landscapes, and generate experiences.

A crypto metaverse, in particular, is one in which the underlying technology is blockchain, and the economy is based on crypto-assets such as metaverse tokens. Different sorts of metaverse tokens are often used to represent crypto assets and goods such as digital land and objects. Their ownership is documented on the blockchain, and they may be traded for digital assets like bitcoin (BTC) and ether (ETH) on a variety of decentralized exchanges (DEXs).

The real world is increasingly migrating to the metaverse. Several companies, both mainstream and crypto-native, have established virtual headquarters in crypto metaverses and host virtual events and festivals that attract thousands of people on a regular basis. For example, in the blockchain game Decentral and, Sotheby's renowned auction company constructed a digital duplicate of its London headquarters in

2021. Metaverse users can visit a multi-room virtual art gallery in the space. Decentral and also conducts live music events, seminars, and meetups on a monthly basis.

The metaverse will require verifiable, immutable ownership of digital products and currencies.

The metaverse is no longer only a sci-fi word. When technology alters our lives, it is not always unexpected. The internet, smartphone, and cloud, to mention a few, all came into the world after a brief appearance in science fiction. The next big thing in the digital era is almost certainly on its way, bringing with it the potential to transform everyday life. It's known as the metaverse.

The metaverse is an amalgamation of virtual reality, augmented reality, and the internet. Its manifestations may be seen in popular video games such as Roblox, Fortnite, and Animal Crossing. The word was originally used in Neal Stephenson's 1992 science fiction novel Snow Crash, in which a couple of delivery couriers journey across the metaverse to escape a capitalist dystopia.

Many futurists envisage a metaverse akin to the ones shown in science fiction films such as Ready Player One.

Users would be able to roam smoothly from place to place with thousands of other individuals, all inside the same digital realm, much like a virtual theme park with no bounds to its size and originality.

Exploring The Metaverse

Today's games, such as Fortnite, Roblox, and Second Life, have the most similarities to the metaverse.

The metaverse will be far more than it is now when it ultimately launches. Once completely created, the metaverse will include three major components:

Interoperability,

presence,

together with standardization

Humans will be able to interact with others electronically and move between virtual environmentsutilizingavatarsandother-digitalobjects.Peoplewilllikelyutilize

cryptocurrencies such as bitcoin (BTC) and Ethereum (ETH) to make payments instead of fiat currency.

The metaverse is projected to alter virtually every sector and give rise to innumerable new business possibilities in its wake. As a result, it may become an interesting region to invest in.

WHY IS THE METAVERSE IMPORTANT

Even if the metaverse falls short of the epic vision that many have for it, it has the potential to dramatically revolutionize the way we interact with the digital world. A collaborative virtual experience, similar to non-fungible tokens (NFT), might open up new options for creators, gamers, and artists, not just restructuring but also inventing the creative economy.

The metaverse's virtual environment might become its own trillion-dollar industry. A destination for entertainment, commerce, and for some, even a place of employment. The metaverse is being referred to as a successor rather than an extension of the internet. The venture capitalist and writer Matthew Ball believe it will be the driving force in the creation of a new generation of firms, similar to how the internet became popular. Perhaps more intriguingly, it may lead to the demise of entrenched sector leaders, as we have seen with the emergence of digital platforms.

Chapter Five

FACEBOOK & METAVERSE

Consider Facebook.

At the end of June, Mark Zuckerberg informed Facebook staff that he would be working to help bring the metaverse to life. The business has formed a team of experts to oversee the initiative, including product chief Vishal Shah and Vivek Sharma, and Jason Rubin from Facebook Gaming.

In an interview with The Verge, Zuckerberg described his vision for the metaverse. He proposed the concept of infinity offices or virtual workplaces. He claims that working in virtual reality allows for better multitasking, and meeting in a virtual, metaverse-like setting can be inherently more collaborative and productive. Zoom calls have clear restrictions, and Zuckerberg has stated that he prefers to do meetings in VR if feasible.

He also mentioned how the metaverse could help solve societal injustices. Based on Raj Chetty's study, Zuckerberg asserts that a person's geographic location is substantially connected with their income potential. However, in a world with a widespread metaverse, this premise is somewhat turned on its head, with remote work becoming more accessible as virtual and augmented reality technology improves.

Facebook intends to lead this development with its own investments. It presently owns Oculus, which manufactures the well-known Quest VR headset. While VR technology is still in its early stages, Zuckerberg believes it will be ready for metaverse capabilities by the end of the decade.

Chapter Six

TECH TITANS VENTURING INTO THE METAVERSE

Other tech titans are venturing into the metaverse.

A single person or corporation cannot control the metaverse, but the typical suspects in the IT industry are already laying their claim to the space's destiny.

Gaming is far ahead of other metaverse technologies in many ways, and it has the potential to lead the way in the future. For years, video games have depended on the notion of in-game economies, in which players may purchase and sell items that have no actual worth outside of the game's realm. The most recent example is Fortnite, but previous examples include the ongoing success of titles such as Grand Theft Auto V.

Despite being published more than seven years ago, the game made more than a billion dollars in profit in 2020 because of a strong online community that is still engaged in the game's online, open-world setting.

Our interaction with it will be more akin to how we interact with the internet than with a virtual role-playing game.

According to Michael Gord, co-founder of the Metaverse Group, skeptics should look at the patterns driven by the epidemic.

The Metaverse Group operates a real estate investment trust that intends to establish a portfolio of assets in Decentral and as well as other worlds such as Somnium Space, Sandbox, and Upland. According to Mr. Gord, there is a notion among investors that there is gold in those pixelated hills.

Imagine coming to New York when it was farmland and having the choice of getting a block of SoHo, he remarked. If someone wants to purchase a block of SoHo real estate today, it's priceless because it's not on the market. That identical event will occur in the metaverse.

Tokens.com secured an even larger property transaction in Decentral and's fashion area for around $2.5 million. According to the corporation, the real estate deal was the largest in metaverse history, and the region would be developed into a virtual commerce hub for premium fashion labels, similar to Rodeo Drive or Fifth Avenue.

Mr. Kiguel believes his metaverse portfolio is worth up to ten times its purchase price, and much of his reasoning will sound familiar to anybody who has ever purchased or sold real estate.

It's all about location, location, location, he explained. A piece of property near the urban center, which receives a high volume of tourist traffic, is more valuable than a parcel of land in the suburbs. There is a value for scarcity.

Many of these digital universes take the form of cartoonish, gummy-colored dream worlds, while others are digital extensions of the reality we already know and love. Owners can purchase plots for emotional or financial reasons, but once they purchase the NFT, they receive a portion of any commerce that occurs on that piece of property.

And when the metaverse penetrates more into our everyday consciousness, a new domain emerges where the line between them has been wiped away: the omniverse.

According to Justin Bannon, co-founder, and CEO of Boson Protocol, which permits the selling of actual objects in the metaverse as NFTs, the real world and the online world blend into one hybrid reality where the fungible and the nonfungible cross at various locations. The metaverse's real estate will hold the commerce that will power this transition.

It's already happening; it's just a matter of degree, he explained. However, I believe that in five years, my daughter would refuse to let me pick her up from school if I am not wearing a pair of sneakers with an NFT.

In June, boson Protocol purchased a full block of Decentral and's Vegas City gaming area. According to the corporation, the area will become a commerce hub where real-world objects can be swapped for NFTs; the same NFTs, which operate as digital representations of tangible products, may also be traded for commodities in physical stores.

Everyone realizes we're really early, and these items will be modern-day antiquities, Mr. Bannon added. Buying at this point is thus quite profitable.

There are just a few digital marketplaces where investors may buy and sell real estate, and they all utilize their own currencies. Decentraland's, for example, is known as MANA. Decentraland also includes a marketplace where users may look for NFTs, such as parcels of land for sale. Mr. Kiguel described it as almost like a multiple listing service.

Wave, an entertainment firm that produces interactive concerts such as Mr. Bieber's, makes money through virtual products and brand sponsorships for the events, which take place in

neutral zones rather than a digital stadium. The firm has not yet monetized real estate, but Adam Arrigo, a co-founder, and CEO stated that he is investigating options.

Platforms like Decentraland and Sandbox are pioneers in authenticating these parcels of property, these shops, he explained. What we do is going to become a lot more mainstream over the next several years.

WHAT CAN YOU ACCOMPLISH IN THE METAVERSE?

What am I able to accomplish in the metaverse?

Every day, the possibilities of what a person can do grow. Exploring the globe, creating a virtual persona, and seeing digital art are currently among the most popular activities. Some digital worlds, such as the Sandbox and Decentraland, allow you to play games or create your own. If you own property in Decentraland, you may host games for yourself and other people to play. Users who have alpha access, or a ticket to a Sandbox test version, can also play games until the test version expires on December 20. You may also participate in activities like virtual casino nights or digital concerts.

If you enjoy virtual shopping, check out Fortune's guide to shopping in the metaverse. Oh, and according to Fortune this week, if you work at a tech-forward corporation, your employer may already be rolling out a return-to-work plan—in the metaverse, of course.

What are you going to do with metaverse land?

Fortune just published an article on an architecture business that assists customers in developing their new land parcels:

Along with those real estate transactions, a new dilemma has emerged: What do you do with a piece of digital property once you've purchased it? One company, Voxel Architects, has turned that idea into a business, designing approximately 40 digital structures this year for customers such as Sotheby's auction house and ConsenSys Software, the inventor of the popular crypto wallet Meta Mask. And business is brisk.

Previously, the business received approximately ten requests for design quotations per week, but that number has risen to about 30 per week, according to George Bileca, chief design officer at Voxel Architects.

According to Leandro Bellone, CEO of Voxel Architects' parent firm NFT Studios, the cost of a project can range from $10,000 to $300,000, depending on the magnitude, amount of capabilities incorporated, and time required to construct it. You may also develop in most of these digital worlds yourself by utilizing the native build program for each platform. On the Sandbox, you can construct structures with its game maker, while on Decentraland, you may construct structures on lands you control using the in-game constructor.

Snoop Dogg, who is developing the Snoop verse on the Sandbox, just sold the rights to be his virtual next-door neighbor for $450,000.

How do you pay for real estate in the metaverse?

If you want to be a landowner, you must first become acquainted with cryptocurrency. Quiroz- Gutierrez explains how to acquire digital real estate in the metaverse in Fortune: Before you buy land, you must first set up a crypto wallet. After downloading Meta Mask (or another type of crypto wallet), you will be prompted to set a password and will most likely be given a secret phrase that you will use to authenticate your identity later. You may use your newly formed crypto wallet to open an account on the Sandbox or Decentraland. Also, remember to investigate a specific metaverse platform before investing in it.

Once you've obtained a wallet, you'll need to convert your US dollars (or whatever money you're using) for a cryptocurrency. Using your debit or credit card, you may quickly acquire Ether, the most often used cryptocurrency for land purchases, through the Meta Mask Google Chrome plugin. To finalize the purchase, Meta Mask will send you to the cryptocurrency exchanges Wire or Transak. Remember that both Wire and Transak charge a fee for changing US dollars to Ether (or other types of cryptocurrencies).

If you need help deciding where to buy land, a slew of brokers and experts have emerged to assist you, including NFT Property Group, MetaMetrics Solutions, and Metaverse Group. Another site that will allow you to scout properties is WeMeta.

POSSIBILITY OF ACQUIRING LAND IN THE METAVERSE

Is it possible to acquire real estate in the metaverse? Yes, there is a land grab taking place.

In a virtual land boom, investors are snapping up Metaverse real estate.

Transactions for real estate in the digital arena are surging, led by the same concept that governs real estate in the physical world: location.

Recently, Justin Bieber played in a live performance, although it was not in a stadium or arena.

Fans from all across the world tuned in to see Mr. Bieber's avatar perform songs from his blockbuster album Justice. Investors were also paying attention. They are buying up music halls, retail complexes, and other properties in the metaverse in preparation for a digital land boom that looks to be just months away.

When Mark Zuckerberg declared last month that Facebook would be known as Meta, an effort to profit on the digital frontier, interest in this digital universe exploded. According to Grayscale, a digital currency investor, the worldwide market for products and services in the metaverse will soon be worth $1 trillion.

The metaverse is made up of several digital domains. Each is similar to a 3-D virtual metropolis in which avatars live, work, and play. Anyone who has played famous video games such as Fortnite, Animal Crossing, or the Roblox world has had a glimpse of what these environments look like.

Technologists predict the metaverse will mature into a fully functional economy in a few years, providing a synchronous digital experience as interwoven into our lives as email and social

networking are now.

Money in these digital worlds is a cryptocurrency since the blockchain powers finance in the metaverse – a digitally distributed public record that eliminates the need for a third party, such as a bank. The NFT acts as proof of ownership and is not interchangeable with other documents.

And in recent months, the pace of transactions for commercial real estate in the metaverse has stepped up.

Tokens.com, a blockchain technology firm focused on NFTs and metaverse real estate, purchased 50% of Metaverse Group, one of the world's first virtual real estate companies, for around $1.7 million in October. Metaverse Group is headquartered in Toronto, but its virtual offices are in a realm named Decentraland in Crypto Valley, the metaverse's counterpart to Silicon Valley. Decentraland also offers gaming, retail, fashion, and arts areas.

Tokens.com has now broken ground digitally on a skyscraper in Decentraland. Louis Vuitton, Gucci, Burberry, and other luxury labels have already entered the metaverse via NFTs, giving firm officials hope that the Tokens.com tower would soon produce money from leasing and advertising for these companies.

ROLE OF CRYPTOCURRENCY IN THE METAVERSE

There will be a need for permissionless identification, financial services, and high-speed trade behind the scenes of the metaverse. Data must be kept and distributed to millions, if not billions, of individuals. The solution to these issues rests in bitcoin technology.

MANA is the money used in Decentraland, and it can be purchased on platforms such as Coinbase. There are even casinos in Decentraland where you may bet in MANA and where the dealers are paid with MANA to show up for work.

The greatest transaction to date was an NFT of a 259-parcel virtual estate in Decentraland, which

sold for more than $900,000.

Interoperable markets will eventually let users purchase and trade virtual commodities from various games and planets. Cryptocurrencies may become the sole legal money in the metaverse, with all virtual objects and intangible items represented by NFTs.

I believe people are actually astounded by the amount of money that gamers invest in digital assets. I believe that converting those assets to NFTs and establishing an NFT economy will add a new layer on top of the present digital economy.

While no one can anticipate precisely what the metaverse will look like or when it will arrive in its ultimate form, the importance of cryptocurrencies to its evolution is undeniable. As we see the evolution of technologies such as virtual reality and how existing industry heavyweights such as Facebook are becoming engaged, improvements in blockchain technology and the cryptocurrency sector will play an equally vital part in molding the metaverse's future.

WAYS TO MAKE A PROFIT IN THE METAVERSE

Investing in the Metaverse: Ways to Make a Profit in the Virtual Future

While the phrase metaverse may be unfamiliar to many, it has been in use for more than three decades. However, it has lately gained appeal as new initiatives begin to surface.

Fans of popular books like Neal Stephenson's Snow Crash or films like Ready Player One or The Matrix know that the metaverse isn't a new notion. For decades, it has been a recurring topic in science fiction. However, the metaverse will no longer be referred to just in science fiction films and novels. The metaverse is on its way to becoming a reality.

But exactly, what is the metaverse? What is it now, and what will it look like in a few years? How many potential investors get started investing in the metaverse? We cover what the metaverse is and how you may obtain investing exposure in this book.

How to Make Money in the Metaverse

If you're a seasoned investor, you know that it's never too late to start investing.

The Metaverse is the current buzzword in the investment world, and here are several methods for investors to obtain exposure to it.

Investing in Metaverse games such as The Sandbox (SAND), Decentraland (MANA), and Axe Infinity is the most direct and cost-effective way to invest in the Metaverse (AXS). To purchase these companies' cryptocurrencies, simply go to crypto exchange like Binance. Simply owning Ethereum is a relatively low-risk approach to acquiring exposure to cryptocurrencies (ETH). As the Metaverse and NFT become increasingly popular, Ethereum will become more extensively utilized, benefiting its value.

Another method to invest in these Metaverse games is to acquire land in The Sandbox or Decentraland through their NFTs. These NFTs may be purchased through sites such as OpenSea via auction or a buy it now option. The disadvantage is that many of the beginning costs for these NFTs are rather high.

Aside from cryptocurrency, there are a few equities that are directly tied to the Metaverse, such as Meta (FB), Roblox (RBLX), and Matterport (MTTR), each with its own distinct promise. Meta, generally known as Facebook, is a social networking platform that also owns VR equipment manufacturer Oculus. Roblox is a game that allows people to communicate and create, whereas Matterport is a firm that uses cameras and software to scan the actual environment in order to create virtual space.

There is also an easier option to buy all Metaverse-related equities by investing in the Metaverse ETF (META), which owns all three stocks mentioned above and will update their holdings on a regular basis based on the company's progress and prospects over time. The ETF carries a 0.75 percent management fee, but it can save investors a significant amount of time and effort.

So, let's get started and look at four different ways you might include the metaverse into your

financial portfolio.

Stocks in the Metaverse

Metaverse ETFs are exchange-traded funds (ETFs)

Tokens in virtual worlds

NFTs in the Metaverse

CHAPTER TWO

Step to step guide to owning digital assets in the metaverse

You may be living in this world now, but there will be others to inhabit shortly (no, we're not talking about Mars). Enter the metaverse, the year's trendiest subject. The word crept into our lives somewhere this year, sometime between the third and whatever pandemic wave we're now in - and it won't leave. This current digital buzz has the usual suspects (read Facebook/Meta, Microsoft, and the rest of Silicon Valley) scrambling for a piece of the action, but smaller businesses are also making a move. But what's the big deal about the metaverse? And what does it have to do with blockchain, NFTs, or living on the internet 24 hours a day, seven days a week? Let's get started since there's a lot to unpack.

To begin with, defining the metaverse is a tall order. We may all agree that there has been a lot of yada, but at the end of the day, would you be able to describe a metaverse to your grandfather over Sunday roast? It can be perplexing since we're discussing something that doesn't yet exist. So, to put it simply, a metaverse is a shared virtual realm that is hyper-realistic, immersive, and interactive due to the utilization of augmented reality (AR) and virtual reality (VR) technologies.

Within a metaverse, there may be multiple virtual worlds where individuals may engage in a variety of activities that are the consequence of a physical and digital combination. Instead of looking at a screen as you do today, you'll be able to be within all of your online experiences, such as shopping and visiting friends and family, attending a performance, and even completing legal documentation in a metaverse.

The metaverse offers numerous significant advantages above what you are currently receiving for your screen time (have you been doing a lot of that lately? We're all guilty of it), so it all

comes down to merging your day-to-day activities into a highly dynamic platform that allows you to get more done in one spot.

The concept of the metaverse had existed since 1992 when Neal Stephenson made up the term metaverse in his dystopian novel called the snow crash. And many of us have seen meta-allusions in pop culture, such as in The Matrix, Ready Player One, or Tron, so the fundamentals of the notion aren't that foreign after all.

In the spirit of getting back to basics, here's a rundown of some of the characteristics that characterize a metaverse:

BOUNDLESS - Because it is a 3D virtual realm, the metaverse removes all physical and other barriers. It's an infinite area with no restrictions on how many people can use it at the same time, what sorts of activities may take place, what industries can enter it, and so on. It provides more accessibility than current internet platforms.

PERSISTENT - A metaverse cannot be disconnected, rebooted, or reset. Users may access it at any time, from wherever in the world, and their experience will always be consistent. A metaverse will change over time depending on the collective contributions of its users, such as the content and experiences they create.

DECENTRALIZED - The metaverse is not controlled by a business or a single platform but by all of its users, who have control over their personal data. Blockchain technology plays an important role in this (more on that later) since it assures that all transactions inside a virtual world are public, readily traced, and secure at all times.

IMMERSIVE - Using a VR headset, AR glasses, or just your smartphone, you'll be able to enter a new level of immersion and interaction, where all human senses are more completely engaged and consumers feel more present in their experiences. The metaverse, as a highly realistic realm, will also be able to adapt to its users, who will be able to directly alter, for example, its settings,

items, colors, lighting, and so on.

VIRTUAL ECONOMIES - Metaverse users can participate in decentralized virtual economies fueled by cryptocurrencies (such as Sensorium Galaxy's own SENSO). This includes markets where users may buy, sell, and trade digital assets like avatars, virtual apparel, NFTs, and event tickets.

SOCIAL EXPERIENCES - The metaverse's beating heart is comprised of its users. Every member in a virtual environment participates in co-experiences and contributes to the metaverse's future through user-generated content, which ranges from virtual creations to personal tales and interactions with AI-driven avatars.

In reality, metaverse-like events existed before Facebook's new Meta rebranding. Earlier incarnations may be seen in games like Second Life and The Sims, where users manage the lives of their online avatars. Even in 2009, Facebook was experimenting in certain pre-metaverse projects, such as Farmville, a game that allowed players to maintain virtual farms and sell their produce in exchange for Farm Coins. And, while these platforms contain components of the metaverse, they are still isolated occurrences with little consequence outside of their native platform.

A real metaverse is a continuous experience that combines components from several media and audiences. Now that we've locked down this component, what else can keep the metaverse ticking?

THE METAVERSE REVOLVES AROUND CRYPTOCURRENCY

Inside the metaverse, anything may happen. And we mean anything since, for the most part, no one knows what the future contains. For the time being, gaming and entertainment are leading the race since they have the most sophisticated infrastructures that can be adopted in a virtual environment and evolve inside it. Their virtual economies are a significant contributor to this.

Take, for example, Roblox, Axie Infinity, or Fortnite. These metaverse-like platforms have achieved enormous popularity, not just because of their entertainment services but also because of their booming markets where users can buy, sell, or trade products in exchange for native tokens like as V-Bucks or AXS. All of these digital-native places rely on a robust virtual economy to generate new assets (such as NFTs), experiences, and activities, which has helped establish the groundwork for metaverse economics.

There is no use in living in a metaverse if the economy cannot sustain its users' activities (and financial goals). As a result, providing value that can be readily monetized is essential for any virtual environment. Remember that many kinds of activities may take place inside the metaverse, and users need a strong enough reason to want to enter and stay in it. Competition, scarcity, supply, and demand are examples of real-world economics that may be applied to any of us.

Blockchain-based currencies enable all assets inside the metaverse to be simply and securely generated, exchanged, shared, and monitored, possibly allowing objects to be smoothly transported across worlds or meta destinations by its users. One SENSO token, for example, is worth $10 per unit inside Sensorium Galaxy. This pricing is applied to customers who purchase SENSO using standard currency payments.

However, SENSO is also sold on crypto exchanges for little more than $2.5 at the time of writing, implying that purchasing SENSO on the open market might give consumers a dynamic discount.

Holding SENSO also provides metaverse users with extra benefits, such as involvement in metaverse governance through a DAO, where users may join the Council and vote on product choices, among other things.

A blockchain-based decentralized economic model bridges the gap between gaming and the metaverse, ushering in a new age of digital-native goods and monetization opportunities. In

contrast to playing a game where all in-platform assets are owned and managed by a developer on a centralized server system, users in the metaverse are the only proprietors of their whole experience. This covers artistic undertakings such as artwork, music, and dance choreographies.

These may be minted as NFTs in metaverses like Sensorium Galaxy and sold in exchange for SENSO in a completely safe environment where ownership and authenticity are always guaranteed via the blockchain.

Blockchains, such as Wakatta, provide another layer of functionality by offering additional forms of NFTs, such as upgradable, time-limited, and text-based NFTs. This makes the metaverse even more fascinating since you will be able to produce NFTs of your work and cooperate with other creators or artists to build on top of existing art without it being unlawful. Wakata's NFTs can also assist metaverse event organizers in tokenizing tickets and game creators in providing in-game assets attached to certain times.

At the end of the day, the metaverse is worth a lot of money. According to some estimations, the yearly income opportunity for virtual worlds might be worth up to $1 trillion, spanning categories such as advertising, digital events, and e-commerce. So, while the metaverse is still mostly underdeveloped, now is not the time to fall asleep at the wheel.

INSIDE THE METAVERSE

Going Inside the Metaverse

So, you've chosen to swallow the red pill and see how deep down the metaverse rabbit hole you can travel. So, what now? To begin, you will require hardware. The good news is that you don't have to go out and buy a piece of high-tech equipment that will most likely set you back a hefty coin. Your smartphone is all you need to access the metaverse, and there are lots of meta-features available right now in Sensorium Galaxy's mobile app, for example. The one caveat is that you

might not receive much of that meta experience after all since you'll miss out on the part of the metaverse, which is what makes it all so wonderful.

A phone is OK for a sneak to peek at, but for the whole experience, you should consider acquiring a VR headset or, if you don't want to go that far, a pair of AR smart glasses. When deciding how to enter a metaverse, there are several factors to consider. Choosing the correct VR headset is going to be one of the essential variables that will make or break your experience. The aim behind using a VR headset instead of other mediums is to become totally immersed in the metaverse and attain a true sensation of presence. Depending on the headset you choose, you'll be able to speak with people via your avatar and activate all of your senses.

Meta (previously Facebook) is well ahead of the competition when it comes to headsets, with its Meta Quest 2 headgear remaining the most popular on the market, followed by PlayStation VR and Valve Index. Demand for VR headsets has increased in recent years, but it is expected to rise much more, no doubt as a result of all the discussion about the metaverse. Apple is also thought to be entering this hotly contested competition.

After a decade of excitement, it appears that both technology and high-quality VR solutions are catching up, and not only in gaming. Applications have sprouted up in a variety of industries, including fashion, music, education, sports, and others, resulting in a significant increase in demand.

This trend is expected to continue as additional platforms transition to virtual reality and, for the first time, enter the metaverse.

Meta is present everywhere.

As previously stated, certain metaverse-like experiences are currently available. Roblox, a video game platform, has experimented with meta events such as commemorating Gucci's 100th anniversary and launching the NFL's first meta store. Meanwhile, competitor Fortnite isn't far

behind, having hosted massively popular virtual concerts, including Ariana Grande, Travis Scott, Marshmallow, and others. However, there are other perspectives on the metaverse's evolution, and some of the current tendencies are expected to continue:

CORPORATE: With a large portion of the world's population shifting to remote work during the COVID-19 epidemic, many of us are already used to working online. The metaverse would just be a continuation of that, as Facebook (sorry, Meta) has already attempted to demonstrate with Horizon Workrooms. Others, such as Microsoft, are following suit, and we can only anticipate more businesses to try to send their employees into the metaverse.

Gaming is enjoyable, and it allows you to make new friends while also earning a lot of money. These platforms are expected to draw the most people to the metaverse because they have a robust social network and a decentralized economy at their heart.

ENTERTAINMENT: Downtime in the metaverse can quickly become extremely different. From chatting with real-life users to making friends with AI-powered avatars to witnessing your favorite acts lead a mind-blowing virtual concert, the metaverse elevates entertainment to a whole new level. Like the metaverse, Sensorium Galaxy, it features a huge musical offering that appeals to a whole universe of fans, thanks to collaborations with some of the world's greatest musicians such as David Guetta, Armin van Buuren, Steve Aoki, and others. Sensorium Galaxy will have other content centers, such as a planet dedicated to meditation and self-actualization techniques, in addition to its music-focused universe.

REAL ESTATE: Are you experiencing a rent crunch? Can't afford to purchase a house? Is there no obvious path out of the rat race? While real-world real estate may be out of reach, purchasing a parcel of virtual land may make you very, very rich. Decentraland just set yet another metaverse record when a 'virtual estate' sold for $2.4 million. And there's lots more to be had in virtual environments like Sandbox. For those looking for more exotic real estate alternatives, you'll be able to locate not just property but also mansions and ships (complete with helipads, hot tubs, and DJ booths).

But, in reality, you can probably discover anything you desire in the metaverse, regardless of your subject of interest. With so many people in the mix, the only limit to the potential of virtual worlds is one's imagination.

METAVERSE VIRTUAL LAND AND HOW TO PURCHASE IT

Intangible land that exists in virtual worlds is referred to as virtual land. It is sold in plots, just like real land, and may be purchased using the money of the specific property. There are now various virtual worlds where you may buy virtual real estate. Decentraland is possibly the most well-known of them.

Virtual estate in the nascent metaverse is fetching hundreds of thousands of dollars.

A plot of property in Decentraland sold for more than USD 900,000 in June of this year. That is only one example. Given the rising interest in the metaverse, the potential ROI (return on investment) on virtual land appears appealing to crypto-savvy investors.

Second, investors may utilize their virtual pieces of land to generate income: if you own a virtual piece of land, you can hold private events or parties and charge people who wish to attend.

For example, American artist Snoop Dogg staged an exclusive party on The Sandbox's non- fungible token (NFT) platform to restore his real-life estate. Attendees needed an NFT, which served as a pass and granted entrance to the event.

Third, investors may earn a consistent income from their virtual lands. For example, you might use NFTs to construct a virtual house on your virtual property and rent it out for a monthly income. Create an NFT art gallery and rent out space to aspiring crypto artists to display their work in the metaverse.

How to Purchase Metaverse Virtual Land

Investing in virtual real estate seemed ludicrous a few years ago. Today's tale is somewhat

different.

Continue reading to discover more about the metaverse and how to invest in virtual real estate to capitalize on the impending metaverse land grab.

The metaverse is increasingly frequently described as an alternate digital world that incorporates virtual reality, augmented reality, and extended reality. Humans will be able to work, play, and live digitally.

The metaverse is a phrase and concept that has been around for over three decades, but it wasn't until recently, after Facebook revealed its aspirations to become a metaverse firm, that the notion gained traction.

As a result, an increasing number of investors are looking for investment possibilities in this rapidly expanding new sector. One of these changes is to purchase virtual land in prominent digital worlds. So let's get started and look at what virtual land is and why investors are interested in it.

When Will You Enter The Metaverse?

A fully formed metaverse might be years away, if not a decade. There are still other technical challenges to solve, beginning with the fact that the globe lacks an internet infrastructure capable of supporting millions of individuals accessing the metaverse at the same time. Furthermore, an uninterrupted and dependable internet connection is a critical component of the metaverse since a glitchy, loaded virtual world situation is far from what a genuine metaverse is meant to look like. However, technology such as 5G and edge computing is still under development and is now incapable of meeting the demands of a sophisticated infrastructure such as the metaverse. There are additional challenges with data privacy and security.

STEP BY STEP GUIDE ON PURCHASING LAND IN DECENTRALAND

Decentraland is a blockchain-powered virtual reality network that allows users to buy land, play games, organize events, and engage with one another in a variety of ways.

It is the most expansive virtual universe in the NFT realm, with its own tokens – MANA and LAND. On Decentraland, each piece of LAND measures 16 meters by 16 meters and is represented by an NFT.

Now that you understand what Decentraland is follow the steps below to learn how to acquire land in Decentraland straight from its Marketplace.

Step 1: Navigate to the Decentralized and Marketplace.

To begin, go to Decentraland's Marketplace and login in or join up if you haven't already. After you've logged in, go to 'Parcels and Estates.' Then, choose 'View All.'

Step 2: Choose a piece of LAND

The next step is to go over the various land parcels and choose your favorite parcel. The benefit of purchasing land in Decentraland straight from the marketplace is that you can observe the surrounding areas as well as the accessibility to renowned sites.

Once you've decided on a piece of virtual land, click on it to learn more about it. The price of the land in MANA, availability, and the name of the owner are all displayed here. To complete the purchase, use the 'Buy' button.

Step 3: Connect your wallet to the Decentraland Marketplace.

To make the purchase, make sure your wallet is linked to your account since the land will be transferred to your wallet as an NFT after the transaction is successful and finished.

If you don't already have a wallet, you can get one by downloading MetaMask or Trust Wallet. Remember that you'll need enough MANA or ethereum (ETH) in your selected wallet to make the purchase. In addition, you'll need some more tokens to cover the gas price.

Step 4: Verify your virtual LAND.

You may confirm your LAND on your wallet after the transaction is completed. You can confirm this in the MetaMask wallet under the 'Collectibles' and 'NFTs' tabs if you use Trust Wallet.

Should You Invest In Metaverse Real Estate?

So far, the virtual real estate market has only known one direction: up.

However, like with any other investment, you should not invest more than you can afford to lose. While there is no doubting that the virtual real estate industry has developed significantly, it is still a relatively young business, and investors should exercise caution and conduct thorough research before investing.

CHAPTER THREE

Crypto gaming

Following its success during the pandemic lockdowns, the gaming business is currently enjoying rapid expansion. In 2020, the UK spent £1.6 billion ($2.1 billion) more on video games than the previous year. People resorted to gaming as a source of home entertainment during the lockdown, from Animal Crossing to Call of Duty.

And it wasn't simply a passing craze. According to investigate research, the worldwide video game sector has expanded this year as well. Private investments more than quadrupled year on year in the first half of 2021, while public offers increased from $4.9 billion in the first half of 2020 to $17.1 billion in H1 2021.

Another trend identified by InvestGame in its research is the emergence of blockchain-based gaming. Crypto games mix the two technologies, whether it's an NFT marketplace or earning bitcoin incentives through gameplay. The use of cryptocurrency in the gaming sector is proving to be a winning combo. One of the most popular crypto games, Axie Infinity, has surpassed a stunning $1.2 billion in earnings.

Because cryptocurrency gaming is gaining a lot of press coverage and investment interest, it's becoming increasingly vital for gaming investors to grasp the specifics of this industry. But, how does cryptocurrency gaming work?

Every year, the internet gambling market is projected to be worth $53.7 billion. There are dozens of ways to stake money through digital casinos, ranging from virtual cards and online sports betting to bingo and video slots. And today, several businesses are giving cryptocurrency games to their clients.

In crypto games, players own the objects they collect and may sell them for cryptocurrency,

which can then be swapped for real money via exchanges.

Cryptocurrency has gotten a lot of attention in a short period of time. Advanced blockchain networks are being developed to benefit the whole industry. While the industry is gaining new and youthful investors, game developers have begun developing blockchain-based games. Continue reading to learn more about what crypto gaming is and how it works.

Blockchain is used in games based on crypto technology. Before one can grasp what crypto gaming is, one must first understand the principle around which such games are founded. Blockchain, at its core, is a database or ledger that stores information by sharing it with a network of computers.

Once information is added to a blockchain, it cannot be changed or withdrawn, making the network extremely secure. Furthermore, the database is accessible to all computers that are linked, ensuring that there is no centralized control of information.

WHAT IS CRYPTO GAMING?

Traditional games are centralized, which means that all objects and experiences (XP) obtained while playing are ineligible for use in other games. By incorporating blockchain technology, crypto gaming has transformed that. Players may now utilize their awards and stuff on many cryptocurrency gaming sites.

Crypto gaming also allows gamers to make money. This is known as a play-to-earn approach, and players can engage in it in a number of ways. Take, for example, Axie Infinity. Users may purchase Axies, level them up, and then sell them for a greater price. Players may also compete with their Axies to gain SLP and AXS, two Ethereum-based crypto gaming currencies.

This offers a completely new aspect to the business - the concept that gamers may earn cryptocurrency while playing games. Worldwide Asset Exchange discovered that this is well-received, as three out of every four gamers expressed a desire to utilize their cash on other

platforms. Is it, however, only gamers who are playing?

Crypto gaming combines online casino games, betting, and cryptocurrency. This implies that you may bet using cryptocurrencies such as Bitcoin, Ethereum, and Dogecoin instead of traditional fiat cash (US dollars, Euros, Pounds Sterling, etc.).

Apart from the money used to fund your account, there are a few distinctions between crypto gambling and traditional online casinos. Most casinos operate in a web browser, but some now have mobile applications, allowing you to play while on the go.

Crypto gaming makes the most sense for those who already trade cryptocurrency. You could wish to gamble anonymously, or you might want to keep your transactions hidden from your bank (or the government). Crypto gaming will most likely remain a fringe passion until cryptocurrencies become more broadly accepted.

Traditional games have a concentrated structure. When characters and other resources are indicated to function with other games, they may do so. Users will be able to transfer their in- game prizes and purchases to other games as well.

WHO CAN PLAY?

Statista records the number of people who have played NFT games in the last 30 days. With over two million monthly users, the top three NFT games are Alien Worlds, Axie Infinity, and Splinterlands.

Although research on crypto gaming demographics is limited, it is evident that gamers are the primary target customers. According to Triple-A, millennials are the largest age group, accounting for 38% of crypto players aged 21 to 38. Fifty-five percent of all millennials who hold crypto money are already gamers.

With 22.6 million players owning cryptocurrencies, Asia-Pacific is a prominent player in this

business. This was followed by 5.9 million Europeans and 5.8 million Middle Eastern and Africans. Surprisingly, North America had the fewest with just 3.3 million crypto players.

This statistic is pretty comparable to that of the overall gaming market. According to Statista, Asia-Pacific nations dominate the top five gaming markets in terms of revenue.

Sergey Kopov is the CEO and creator of 0xGames, a blockchain game development firm that has worked on several projects. He expects that crypto gaming would appeal to the gaming industry's

3.24 billion global users.

Crypto games primarily attract not gamers but those who want to profit from this new craze, Kopov explained. This, however, is just transitory. Soon, crypto games will be fascinating enough to compete with classic games on the gaming field, attracting gamers' attention.

The Philippines has emerged as a cryptocurrency gambling hotspot. The Covid epidemic significantly impacted the country's economy, but some citizens discovered a new method to generate money. A documentary follows Filipinos who made money on Axie Infinity, demonstrating that there is money to be gained by investing time in these sites. The documentary also addressed the notion of cryptocurrency gamers. It included a mother, a fresh college graduate, a cab driver, and an older married couple who were cryptocurrency players.

It is really simple to get started with crypto gaming. All you need is a bitcoin wallet and an account with a gambling site that accepts cryptocurrencies. Also, A gaming device, such as a smartphone, tablet, or computer.

For a skilled web user, setting up the wallet and gaming account is quick and uncomplicated - and there are several free tutorials to assist. The main difficulty may be in selecting a gaming device - some games may demand high-performance computing power to function effectively. Your gaming experience may suffer if your smartphone is more than a year or two old.

CRYPTO GAMES: SUCCESSFUL ONES

Because the game has Asian roots, it is not surprising that Axie Infinity has gained popularity in the Philippines. Trung Nguyen, a Vietnam-based game developer, established Sky Mavis, which debuted the Ethereum-based game. Sky Mavis's valuation is presently well about $3 billion as of December 2021, which is particularly amazing given that the firm obtained $152 million in startup investment from crypto investors in October 2021.

Despite its high worth, Axie Infinity is only the second most popular cryptocurrency game, trailing Alien Worlds, which has over 700,000 daily users. Saro McKenna, the game's co-founder, has corporate finance experience and has worked for ten years. She also has a master's degree from Oxford University.

Despite the fact that Alien Worlds is more popular than Axie Infinity, the in-game money reveals a different picture. As of the 8th of December, the Axie Infinity token (AXS) is valued at

$107.91 and ranks first among all cryptocurrencies in terms of market capitalization. On the other hand, alien Worlds (TLM) is ranked 292nd and costs only $0.24.

Splinterlands, a blockchain card game, is ranked third on Statista's list, with around 600,000 weekly participants. You may buy, trade, and level up cards in the game. Matthew Rosen, the creator, and chief technical officer of Splinterlands in Philadelphia, has been making video games since he was ten years old.

Splintershards (SPS) is the card game's token, which is presently valued at $0.36. Although the price is greater than TLM, the market capitalization is lesser, and it is ranked 415 on CoinMarketCap.

With over 700,000 monthly players, Alien Worlds is the most popular crypto game, while Axie Infinity's coin AXS has a bigger market capitalization. AXS is now valued at $107.91, while Alien World's TLM is priced at $0.24.

HOW DO CRYPTO GAMES WORK?

Many components of crypto alternatives are already present in traditional games. Players may buy in-game money using fiat cash, gather things, and level up their characters. So, what draws investors and gamers to cryptocurrency gaming?

Ownership is one of the reasons why crypto gaming has grown in popularity. The marketplace dynamic has intrigued players, whether it is a Splinterlands creature card or a purple Axie with green thorns.

Earning money through gaming is also appealing to gamers. Certain games have previously been chastised for employing a pay-to-play paradigm, in which users must invest money in order to get the most out of a game. Previously, putting money in crypto gaming would merely improve your experience, such as being able to level up faster. On the other hand, Crypto gaming achieves the opposite: the play-to-earn paradigm now allows players to benefit from their investment in crypto gaming tokens. Some gamers in the Philippines have even been able to earn a living as a result of this.

In conventional gaming and development, developers control all digital assets such as XP, in- game cash, weapons, skins, characters, automobiles, and so on. In contrast, in a crypto game, the user owns the goods obtained as the game progresses. Because such games are produced on blockchain networks, all linked computers have access to the same amount of information (all of it), decentralizing information control and offering equal rights and controls to players and producers. Blockchain technology may be used in crypto games for two objectives. The creators may either build the entire game on a blockchain or merely utilize it for in-game cash. In the first example, every activity inside the game is confirmed and saved as new blocks in the blockchain.

Non-fungible tokens, or NFTs, can be utilized for in-game digital assets in the second situation.

Investors may participate in crypto games in a variety of ways. Some crypto game tokens, such as AXS, may be purchased on exchanges such as Binance. Investors are also welcome to participate in financing rounds. Sky Mavis, Animoca, and Enjin are three blockchain-based game startups that have recently raised capital. The most apparent approach to participating is

investing time in playing and receiving crypto tokens as incentives.

Remember that cryptocurrencies are volatile, so conduct your own research before investing, and never invest more than you can afford to lose.

RISKS OF CRYPTO GAMING

Despite its benefits, crypto gaming has its own set of issues. There are certain games that are more difficult to access than others. Axie Infinity, for example, requires users to obtain three Axies before they may participate. The cheapest Axies are roughly $100, so you'll need to spend at least $300 before you can start earning. The ordinary player may be thrown off by the high amount of investment, as most traditional games do not cost more than $100.

You also run the danger of losing your tokens and NFTs. This can occur if you attempt to send them to a wallet that does not accept the NFT kind or if you fall victim to fraud. This is not uncommon; in July, the inventor of the crypto game Hedgie was duped out of about $1 million in NFTs.

This is an even greater danger for crypto games than it is for cryptocurrencies because operators are not normally required to comply with certain regulations, such as anti-money laundering, which can raise the chance of fraud.

In addition to malicious attempts, players might lose money due to volatility. Cryptogame tokens, like non-gaming cryptocurrencies, are subject to price fluctuations, although some games limit the number of times you may withdraw tokens. This implies that if a crypto gaming coin like AXS declines in value, users may not have enough time to cut their losses.

Combining two of the most advanced technologies exacerbates a critical problem that both are vulnerable to gambling. Loot boxes are a new feature in video games that allows players to pay to open a virtual box containing random things. According to one study, treasure boxes are structurally and cognitively similar to gambling.

Loot boxes have also made an appearance in cryptocurrency games. Splinterlands, for example, offers you to purchase packs of random cards. With gaming's millennial user base, health experts are afraid that gambling has become a part of young people's everyday lives, and crypto gaming will further feed this.

Cryptocurrencies operate outside of regular financial institutions, which means they are immune to many of the safeguards provided by banks. If a hacker gains access to your account, most banks provide some type of insurance to ensure your money is safe.

If a hacker gains access to your bitcoin wallet, there are no safeguards in place — nor is there any means to recover your funds. You must exercise extreme caution to ensure that your wallet and crypto gaming accounts are adequately safeguarded from loss or theft. You should also be aware that the safeguards provided by crypto gaming service providers may be rather minimal. Examine the terms of service to determine whether they provide any compensation if hackers breach their systems.

FUTURE OF CRYPTO GAMING

Crypto gaming is becoming increasingly popular, and investors want to be a part of it. Sky Mavis secured $7.5 million in its first round of fundraising thanks to Mark Cuban's investment. Venture capital firms are also getting in on the act, with Bitkraft Ventures launching a $75 million fund for crypto gaming businesses.

Blockchain firms are also interested, and Solana and Polygon have begun investing in early-stage blockchain games that include decentralized financing (DeFi) into their systems. With more and more investors putting their money into crypto gaming platforms, the sector might see a boom.

However, in October, the crypto gaming sector suffered a huge setback when Steam, the world's largest distributor of PC games, stated that the platform would not host blockchain-based games, ostensibly because it will not accept products with real-world value on its platform. Loss of

Steam support might have a big impact on crypto games, as they would lose access to an industry-leading marketplace with 62.6 million daily users.

Epic Games, the distributor, is adopting a different strategy. Although Epic will not be releasing its own crypto games, CEO Tim Sweeney stated on Twitter that the company is eager to collaborate with early creators on their blockchain-based games. According to the video game distributor, crypto games must comply with financial regulations and have acceptable age ratings. This might eliminate many of the hazards associated with crypto games while also opening up the market to Epic Games' 31.3 million daily players.

Capital.com analyst Mikhail Karkhalev stated on the future of crypto games, Attracting the young generation to the crypto sector through games that also create revenue is a key growth driver for the crypto market. Given the increased labor market rivalry and significant unemployment as a result of the epidemic, the ability to make respectable money by playing games is essentially a lifesaver for people in underdeveloped nations.

CHAPTER FOUR

Future of blockchain technology concerning the metaverse

Today's cryptocurrency investors are expected to dominate the metaverse, also known as web 3.0, which has the ability to revolutionize how we live, engage, and conduct business.

My forecast comes as the race between technology firms to develop the metaverse has officially begun. Facebook stated at the end of last month that it was reorganizing and adopting the corporate name Meta, stating that from now on, we're going to be metaverse-first, not Facebook- first. In addition, the internet behemoth plans to hire 10,000 individuals in the European Union to work on its new project.

The phrase metaverse refers to a virtual counterpart to physical reality in which a community of individuals can interact as avatars. It is the combination of physical, augmented, and virtual reality in a shared online environment.

Facebook's statement emphasizes even again that the metaverse is being viewed as the internet's successor, not as an 'extension.'

It will become the gateway to nearly all digital experiences and an essential component of the majority of physical ones, significantly altering the way we live, engage with one another, and conduct business.

It will revolutionize economies and be the key to the formation of entire new generations of enterprises, which is why the large tech giants are stepping in — no one wants to be left behind something so important.

The metaverse is constructed and powered by blockchains and decentralized apps, the same

cutting-edge technology that powers cryptocurrencies such as Bitcoin and Ethereum.

Chapter Seven

CREATING THE METAVERSE

Who else has the ability to create the Metaverse?

Although the Metaverse can replace the internet as a computing platform, its evolutionary path will most certainly differ from that of its predecessor. Private enterprise is not only fully aware of the Metaverse's promise, but it also has the most aggressive belief in its future, not to mention the most money, the greatest engineering talent, and the most conquering desire. The most powerful technological corporations want to own and define the Metaverse, not just lead it.

Open-source initiatives with a non-corporate approach will continue to be important in the Metaverse, attracting some of the fascinating creative individuals. However, there were only a few prospective leaders in the early Metaverse, including Microsoft, Apple, Meta..

Microsoft's Mesh platform is one of the metaverse crypto initiatives. The US Army is apparently working with Microsoft on an augmented reality Hololens 2 headgear for soldiers to train, rehearse, and battle in. Furthermore, Xbox Live connects millions of video game players from across the world.

While Apple has lagged behind firms like Meta and others in introducing the first AR and VR devices, the Cupertino company may not be too far behind. For the next Metaverse, Apple has developed a powerful HMD (Head Mounted System) Virtual Meetings software. Apple's patent also covers a number of methods that allow individuals to perceive and interact with augmented reality (ER) settings.

Metaverse

Depending on the source, there are several definitions and perspectives on the metaverse.

It is defined as a virtual-reality arena in which users may interact with a computer-generated environment and other users by the Oxford Dictionary.

The metaverse, according to Mark Zuckerberg at Connect 2021, is a virtual reality construct meant to displace the internet, connect virtual life with the real world, and create unlimited new playgrounds for everyone – you'll be able to do practically anything you can think.

NFTs

A non-fungible token (NFT) is an intangible digital asset such as photographs, video, or game goods.

These virtual assets come with certificates that prove ownership and have an impact on the metaverse's progress. NFTs are purchased and traded with cryptocurrencies such as Bitcoin.

What Is A Simple Way To Begin Using NFTs?

Create a wallet (such as MetaMask or Venly), convert fiat cash (dollars) to Etherum or Hedera

(crypto), and purchase an NFT.

The same is true for artists, but you will also be able to mint NFTs on the blockchain. But watch out for those annoying petrol costs!

3.0 Web

Web3, also known as Web 3.0, is the third generation of the Internet. It is a decentralized version of the Internet that does not rely on Google, Facebook, or Twitter.

It is seen as the next technological revolution since it mixes machine learning and big data and is expected to provide a personalized and private experience.

The old Facebook had made significant investments in virtual reality, including the 2014 acquisition of Oculus. Meta envisions a virtual world in which digital avatars communicate with one another via virtual reality headsets for business, travel, or recreation.

However, we don't know enough about the Metaverse to form strong ideas on who will lead it or how they will bring us there. In actuality, the Metaverse is most likely the consequence of a network of various platforms, entities, and technologies working and embracing interoperability (although unwillingly).

The internet as we know it today emerged through a rather tumultuous process in which the open (mostly academic) internet coexisted with closed (largely consumer-oriented) services that frequently tried to rebuild or reset open standards and protocols.

What is the maximum size of the metaverse?

Some of us are old enough to recall Second Life, the SIMS-like virtual environment that captivated people's minds for a brief period in the 2000s. Despite the fact that it never became popular, it nevertheless maintains a passionate following. But the dynamics at work two decades later, not to mention the massive technological advances in the intervening years, promise to make the metaverse much more than a niche product.

How can you safeguard your metaverse investment?

If you own a house, you undoubtedly have insurance and maybe a security system in the real world. For the time being, the best thing you can do to safeguard your metaverse assets is to utilize a hardware wallet. A hardware wallet is a physical USB stick that you may use to safeguard your land from phishing attempts by incorporating two-step authentication for any cash or NFTs transferred out of your wallet. You may also utilize the disk to safely access the land and sell it from any computer in the globe, adding an added degree of security, Quiroz- Guiterrez writes.

BRANDS USING THE METAVERSE

How are brands making use of the metaverse?

There is already a buying binge in progress. According to Bloomberg, labels such as Gucci, Balenciaga, and Burberry are creating virtual worlds where customers can explore, shop, and hang out: Big names have already staked their mark in the metaverse. For example, the Gucci Garden, a Roblox pop-up that sold the brand's goods, saw one bag earn $4,000 in real-world dollars. Nike Inc., too, announced a deep collaboration with the platform to establish Nikeland, a virtual environment patterned after the company's headquarters in Oregon that sells unique merchandise. Balenciaga released a Fortnite clothing line in September. These skins, or clothes for game avatars, are purchased using V Bucks, the Fortnite world's money. (V Bucks require actual money to get.).

How Are Brands Making Their Way Into The Metaverse?

It appears that virtual reality and augmented reality (AR) are the emerging frontiers in digital marketing.

Vstores, or virtual showrooms, are being built by brands to allow customers to take a tour, engage with a place, or interact with 3D objects such as vehicles, jewelry, or any digital asset.

Customers will be able to use augmented reality to try on glasses or cosmetics, as well as picture furniture and other things in their homes, thanks to virtual try-on.

Increase the Effectiveness of Your Content by Using Keyword Intent Analysis

It's never been simpler to rapidly connect your keywords with the proper audience and content, thanks to Semrush's keyword intent meter.

Innovative marketers are transforming concerts, art festivals, and athletic events into digital experiences.

Avatars require a fashion budget.

Selling virtual reality digital representations of things is emerging as a new business stream.

Gucci, Nike, and Dior all provide digital items that allow avatars to be personalized and customized, such as purses, shoes, hats, and sunglasses, because avatars now require wardrobe changes based on events, seasons, and emotions.

Going direct to the avatar (D2A) is a business approach in which marketers sell to digital identities directly.

In a digital environment, there are no transportation or supply chain concerns to deal with while designing, developing, and selling. Individuals can experiment with their digital selves to discover their identities.

Brands pressed the play button, and the game began. It's a form of meta-branding.

Event sponsorship has a proven ROI in the physical world, and this classic marketing approach is easily transferable to the metaverse.

Gamifying commerce entails adding more innovation to the competition.

Louis Vuitton, for example, produced a video game to engage a younger audience and gamified it with branded NFT artifacts.

Nike employs 3D technology to allow customers to construct/design their items while also gaining vital intelligence by allowing fans to make their own sneakers.

Virtual pop-ups enable interaction from a distance.

Using virtual worlds with brand placement to generate a creative and customized opportunity, especially in post-pandemic periods, creates a creative and customizable opportunity.

Coach, Disney, and Keith Haring collaborated on a fashion, lifestyle, and art exhibition.

The three created a virtual pop-up shop where visitors could explore and purchase limited edition

physical and digital presents.

The digital shop included Mickey's ears, shearling coats, totes, and sweatshirts emblazoned with Haring's unique artwork, as well as AR filters and a custom Spotify playlist.

Talk about contradictory reality and experiences.

Try-on in a Snap to reduce returns and increase direct sales.

Snap provides advertisers with the option to use Snap's AR platform to engage Snapchatters in try-on with shoes, sunglasses, hats, and other items.

They can buy the goods right away if they like them. Gucci created a case study to demonstrate this.

As Snapchatters purchased things from the app, the shopping AR experience created positive ROAS! Not bad for a campaign that was solely meant to raise awareness and interaction, Snap says.

GUIDE TO NON FINANCIAL TRANSACTIONS AND THE METAVERSE

The Metaverse is brimming with prospects for companies and marketers who are familiar with AR/VR and NFT. Find out who's already there and how to get started.

Consider your avatar entering a digital wine shop and conversing with an avatar wine specialist to get some queries addressed.

You order the wine and have it delivered to your home location. Welcome to the metaverse, the nexus of our digital and physical worlds. Is your brand ready for NFTs, the metaverse, and web 3.0?

We'll go over some terminology, the current potential for brands in the metaverse, and how to get started in this area.

Along the way, you'll find advice, examples, and a wealth of tools to assist you in developing your own metaverse marketing plan.

Important Meta Marketing Terminology

First, let's be clear about what we're talking about.

CPSIA information can be obtained
at www.ICGtesting.com
Printed in the USA
BVHW060050220722
642761BV00006B/388